I'm a Little Teapot

A Doubleday Book for Young Readers

A Doubleday Book for Young Readers
Published by Delacorte Press
Bantam Doubleday Dell Publishing Group, Inc.
666 Fifth Avenue
New York, New York 10103

This edition was first published in Great Britain in 1990 by Hutchinson Children's Books, Random Century Group Ltd.

Library of Congress Cataloging in Publication Data
McGee, Shelagh.
I'm a little teapot : games, rhymes, and songs for the first three years / Shelagh McGee.
p. cm.
Summary: Teaches games to play while reciting favorite nursery rhymes.
ISBN 0-385-30324-6
1. Games – Juvenile literature. 2. Nursery rhymes, English – Juvenile literature.
3. Children's songs. [1. Games. 2. Finger play. 3. Nursery rhymes. 4. Songs.]
I. Title.
GV1203.M354 1992
793'.01922 dc20
90-49072 CIP AC

Manufactured in Hong Kong
June 1992

10 9 8 7 6 5 4 3 2 1
CHU

I'm a Little Teapot

Games, Rhymes, and Songs
for the First Three Years

SHELAGH McGEE

A Doubleday Book for Young Readers

ENCOURAGE
BROTHERS AND SISTERS
TO SING TO BABY.

Bye, baby bunting
Daddy's gone a-hunting,
He's gone to fetch a rabbit skin,
To wrap his baby bunting in,
Bye, baby bunting.

Golden slumbers kiss your eyes,
Smile awake when you arise.
Sleep, pretty baby, do not cry,
And I will sing a lullaby:
Rock them, rock them, lullaby.

THE RHYTHM OF A SIMPLE RHYME CAN SOOTHE BABY—
AND YOU AS WELL.

Rock-a-bye baby in the treetop,
When the wind blows, the cradle will rock,
When the bough breaks, the cradle will fall,
Down will come baby, cradle and all.

PLAY A GAME OF PEEKABOO,
HIDING BEHIND YOUR HANDS OR A SCARF.

Peekaboo, baby,
Look and see,
One, two, three,
Boo! It's me!

Lavender's blue, dilly dilly,
Lavender's green,
When I am King, dilly dilly,
You shall be Queen.

Hush, little baby, don't say a word,
Papa's going to buy you a mockingbird.
And if that mockingbird don't sing,
Papa's going to buy you a diamond ring.
And if that diamond ring turns to brass,
Papa's going to buy you a looking glass.
And if that looking glass gets broke,
Papa's going to buy you a billy goat.
And if that billy goat runs away,
Papa's going to buy you another someday.

RHYMES CAN MAKE BATHTIME ROUTINE ENJOYABLE.

Doctor Foster
Went to Gloucester
In a shower of rain.
He stepped in a puddle
Right up to his middle
And never went there again.

Hoddley, poddley, puddle and frogs,
Cats are to marry the poodle dogs,
Cats in blue jackets and dogs in red hats,
What will become of the mice and the rats?

SAY THIS RHYME WHILE TOWELING DRY OR SPLASHING AND SPONGING.

Tickle, ickle, ickle,
Little, little pickle,
Here's a little tickle,
Tick, tick, tick.

Chickle, ickle, ickle,
Little, little chicken,
Have a little chuckle,
Chuck, chuck, chuck.

TICKLE TUMMY, PALMS, AND FEET.

A RHYME TO SAY AT NAPTIMES . . . OR MEALTIMES.

"Let's go to bed," says Sleepyhead,
"Let's stay awhile," says Slow,
"Put on the pan," says Greedy Nan,
"Let's eat before we go."

Heave ho! Heave ho!
Hold me tight
Don't let me go.
One two, one two,
You love me
And I love you.

PULL BABY VERY GENTLY BY THE ARMS
TO RAISE HIM FROM THE MAT.

Jack, be nimble,
Jack, be quick,
Jack, jump over
The candlestick.

SWING A TOY TO AND FRO—
BABY'S EYES WILL FOLLOW IT.

Here we go looby loo,
Here we go looby light,
Here we go looby loo,
All on a Saturday night.

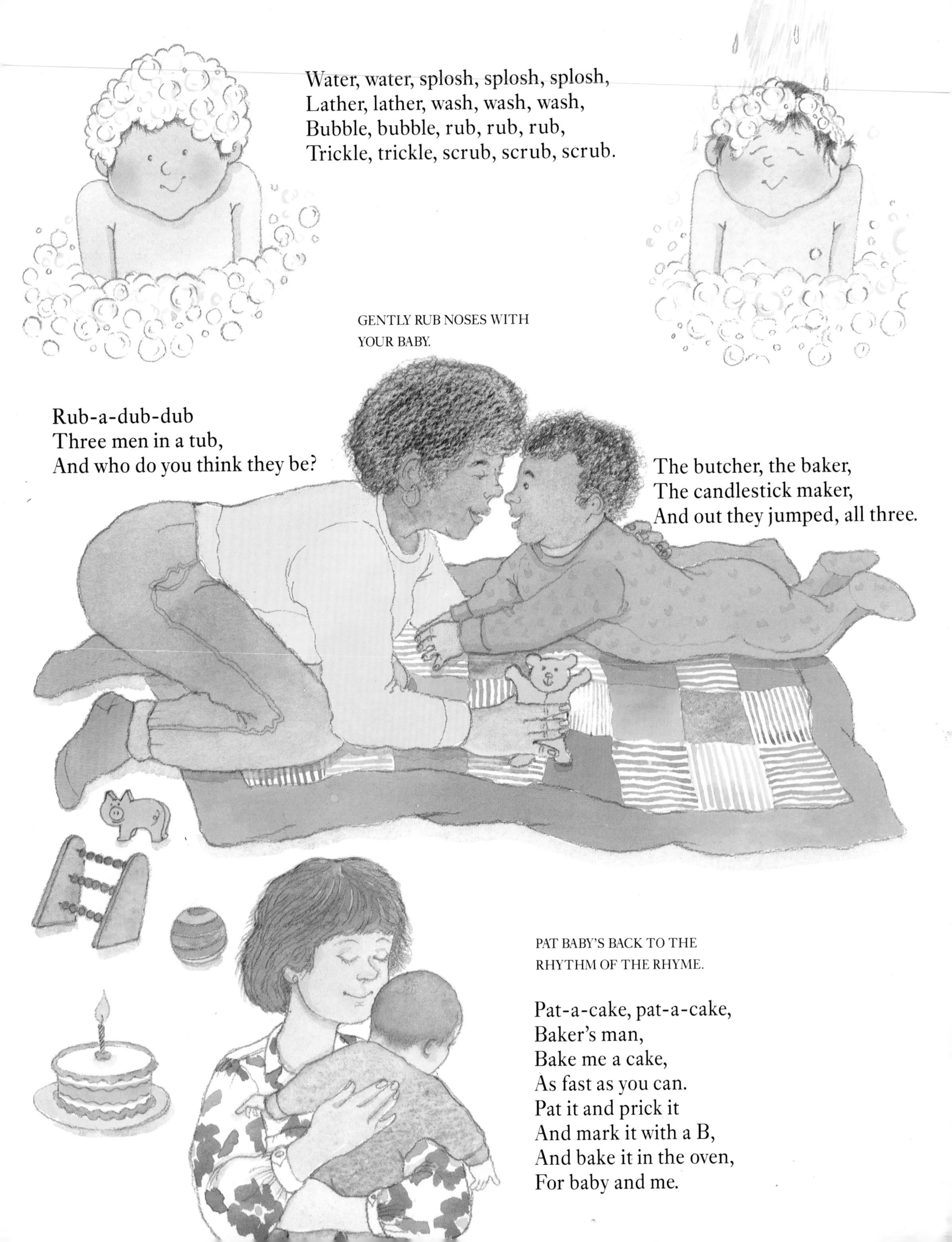

Water, water, splosh, splosh, splosh,
Lather, lather, wash, wash, wash,
Bubble, bubble, rub, rub, rub,
Trickle, trickle, scrub, scrub, scrub.

GENTLY RUB NOSES WITH YOUR BABY.

Rub-a-dub-dub
Three men in a tub,
And who do you think they be?

The butcher, the baker,
The candlestick maker,
And out they jumped, all three.

PAT BABY'S BACK TO THE RHYTHM OF THE RHYME.

Pat-a-cake, pat-a-cake,
Baker's man,
Bake me a cake,
As fast as you can.
Pat it and prick it
And mark it with a B,
And bake it in the oven,
For baby and me.

CLAP BABY'S HANDS, STRETCH LEGS,
THEN PULL GENTLY AGAINST FEET TO BEND KNEES.

Baby, baby, clap your hands,
Smile your smile so sweet.
Bend your knees
And stretch your legs,
Let's tickle little feet.

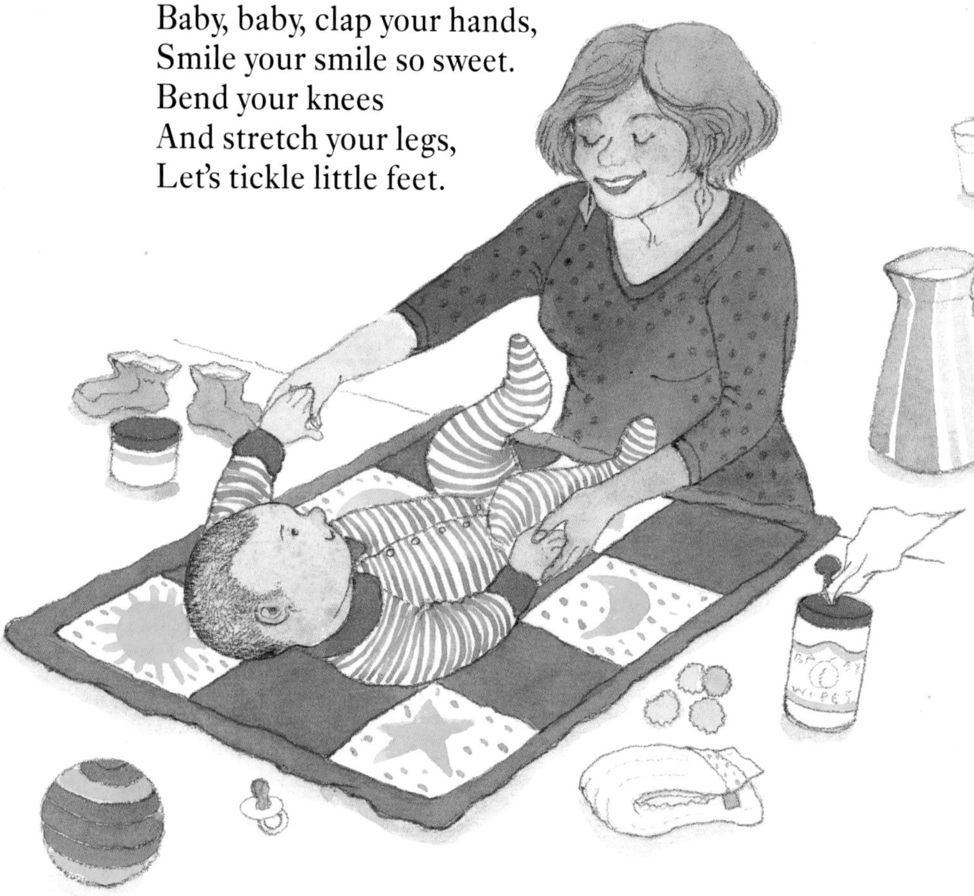

A RHYME FOR
CLAPPING TO.

Clap hands, Daddy come,
Bring his baby a sugar bun,
Stamp feet, Mommy here,
Bringing baby ginger beer.

CRAWL WITH YOUR BABY
WHILE SAYING THIS RHYME.

"Pussycat, pussycat,
Where have you been?"
"I've been to London
To visit the Queen."
"Pussy cat, pussy cat,
What did you there?"
"I frightened a little mouse
Under the chair."

YOUR BABY WILL ENJOY YOUR BEING DOWN ON HIS LEVEL.

This little piggy went to market,
This little piggy stayed home,
This little piggy had roast beef,
This little piggy had none,
And this little piggy went, "Wee! Wee! Wee!"
All the way home.

WIGGLE EACH TOE IN TURN AND
TICKLE ALL THE WAY HOME.

YOUR LEG IS THE HORSE—
GENTLY JOG YOUR BABY UP AND DOWN
TO THE RHYTHM OF THE RHYME.

Ride a cockhorse
To Banbury Cross,
To see a fine lady
Upon a white horse.
Rings on her fingers
And bells on her toes,
She shall have music
Wherever she goes.

Cock-a-doodle-doo!
My dame has lost her shoe,
My master's lost his fiddling stick,
Oh, what are they to do?

A RHYME FOR GETTING DRESSED OR UNDRESSED TO.

Diddle, diddle, dumpling,
My son John,
Went to bed with his trousers on,
One shoe off and one shoe on,
Diddle, diddle, dumpling,
My son John.

USE YOUR ARMS AS THE HANDS OF THE CLOCK
AND MOVE THEM AROUND WITH EACH LINE OF THE RHYME.

Clock strikes one,
All alone,
Clock strikes two,
For me and you.
Clock strikes three,
Let's have tea,
Clock strikes four,
Time for more.

This is the way we clean our teeth,
Clean our teeth, clean our teeth,
This is the way we clean our teeth
On a cold and frosty morning.

MAKE ENERGETIC BRUSHING MOVEMENTS
FOR YOUR CHILD TO COPY.

This is the way we wash our hands,
Wash our hands, wash our hands,
This is the way we wash our hands
On a cold and frosty morning.

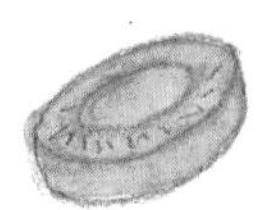

This is the way we brush our hair,
Brush our hair, brush our hair,
This is the way we brush our hair
On a cold and frosty morning.

This is the way we shine our shoes,
Shine our shoes, shine our shoes,
This is the way we shine our shoes
On a cold and frosty morning.

IF BABY DOESN'T EAT UP HIS DINNER
THE FOX WILL GRAB IT!

Quick! Quick!
Can I come in?
A fox is after me.
Quick! Quick!
Fast as you can.
He's looking for his tea.

PAT YOUR TUMMY WHILE
SAYING THE RHYME.

Hot cross buns,
Hot cross buns,
One a penny, two a penny,
Hot cross buns.
If you have no daughters,
Give them to your sons.
One a penny, two a penny,
Hot cross buns.

TRY BALANCING SOMETHING
ON YOUR HEAD, PRETENDING
IT'S A KETTLE.

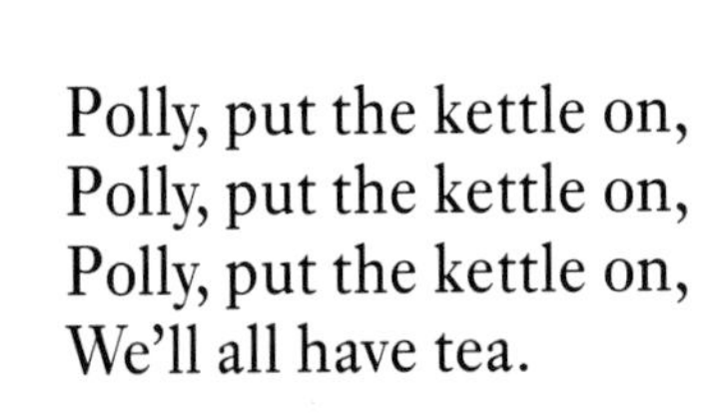

Polly, put the kettle on,
Polly, put the kettle on,
Polly, put the kettle on,
We'll all have tea.

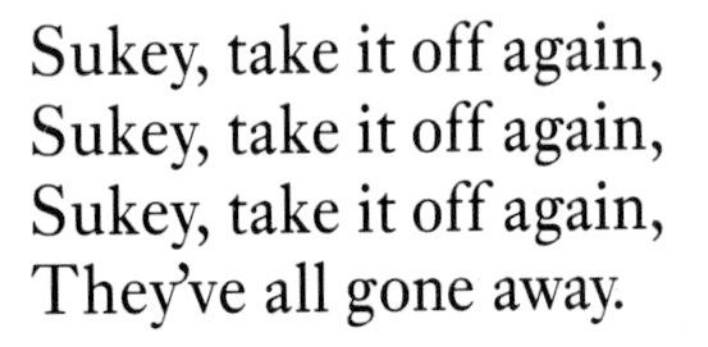

Sukey, take it off again,
Sukey, take it off again,
Sukey, take it off again,
They've all gone away.

MAKE SEESAW MOVEMENTS WITH YOUR ARMS
AND GET YOUR CHILD TO COPY YOU—FASTER, FASTER, AND FASTER.

Seesaw, Margery Daw,
Johnny shall have a new master.
He shall have but a penny a day,
Because he won't work any faster.

Round and round the garden,
Like a teddy bear.
One step, two steps,
Tickle you under there!

DO THE TRADITIONAL FINGER RHYME IN YOUR BABY'S PALM . . . ENDING WITH A TICKLE!

CHILD PATS HIS TUMMY AT EACH MENTION OF THE MUFFIN MAN.

Have you seen
The muffin man,
The muffin man,
The muffin man?
Have you seen
The muffin man
Who lives down
Drury Lane?

Yes, I've seen
The muffin man,
The muffin man,
The muffin man,
Yes, I've seen
The muffin man
Who lives down
Drury Lane.

MAKE A FIST FOR EACH "POTATO,"
PILING THEM ONE ON TOP OF THE OTHER AS YOU COUNT.

One potato, two potato,
Three potato, four,
Five potato, six potato,
Seven potato, more!

BOUNCE YOUR CHILD UP AND DOWN GENTLY FOR THE FIRST VERSE, REALLY VIGOROUSLY FOR THE SECOND.

To market, to market,
To buy a fat pig,
Home again, home again,
Jiggety, jig!
To market, to market,
To buy a fat hog,
Home again, home again,
Jiggety, jog!

Georgie Porgie, pudding and pie,
Kissed the girls and made them cry,
When the boys came out to play,
Georgie Porgie ran away.

KISS NOSE, THEN TICKLE ALL OVER AS GEORGIE PORGIE RUNS AWAY.

ENCOURAGE YOUR CHILD TO COPY OR INVENT CREEPY-CRAWLY MOVEMENTS.

The itsy-bitsy spider
Climbed up the water spout,
Down came the rain
And washed the spider out.
Out came the sun
And dried up all the rain,
And the itsy-bitsy spider
Climbed up the spout again.

ALWAYS TRY TO RESCUE LADYBUGS,
SPIDERS, ANTS, AND PILL BUGS,
AND PUT THEM OUTSIDE IF YOU CAN.

Ladybug, ladybug,
Fly away home,
Your house is on fire,
Your children have gone,
All except one,
And that's little Ann,
And she's hiding under the frying pan.

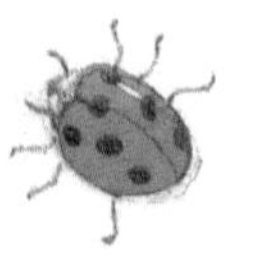

Bobby Shafto's gone to sea,
Silver buckles at his knee,
When he comes back he'll
marry me,
Bonny Bobby Shafto.

Bobby Shafto's tall and fair,
Combing out his golden hair,
He's my love forevermore,
Bonny Bobby Shafto.

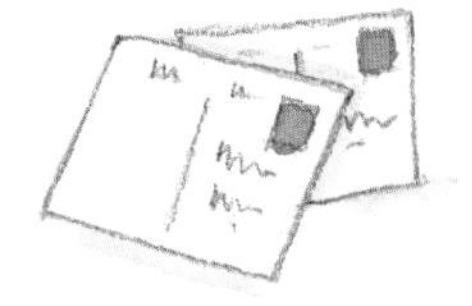

SLAP YOUR KNEES AS YOU SAY THE RHYME . . . LOOK OUT TO SEA

Twinkle, twinkle, little star,
How I wonder what you are,
Up above the world so high,
Like a diamond in the sky.
Twinkle, twinkle, little star,
How I wonder what you are.

POINT UP TO THE SKY. LOOK FOR STARS AT BEDTIME.

AN EXCELLENT TICKLING RHYME.

Hickory, dickory, dock,
The mouse ran up the clock.
The clock struck one,
The mouse ran down,
Hickory, dickory, dock.

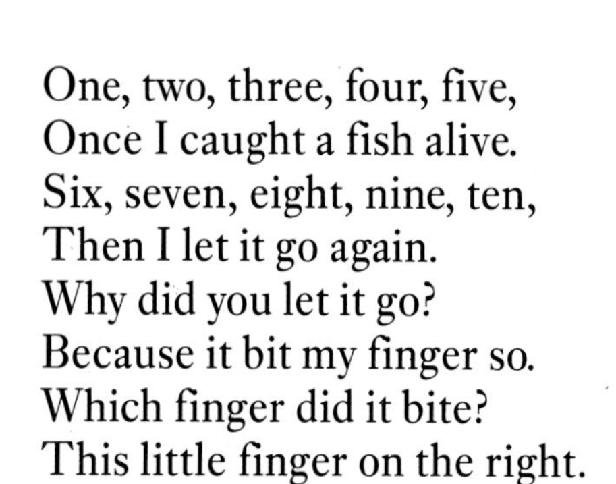

One, two, three, four, five,
Once I caught a fish alive.
Six, seven, eight, nine, ten,
Then I let it go again.
Why did you let it go?
Because it bit my finger so.
Which finger did it bite?
This little finger on the right.

COUNT EACH FINGER.

PULL EACH OTHER BACK AND FORTH IN A ROWING MOTION TO THE RHYTHM OF THE RHYME.

Row, row, row your boat,
Gently down the stream.
Merrily, merrily, merrily, merrily,
Life is but a dream.

Eeny, meeny, miny, mo,
Catch my baby by his toe,
If he squeals, let him go,
Eeny, meeny, miny, mo.

START WITH THE LITTLE TOE, "CATCH" THE TWO BIG TOES, THEN EENY MEENY TO THE OTHER LITTLE TOE.

SAY THIS RHYME WHEN BRUSHING YOUR HAIR.
SEE WHO CAN MAKE THE MOST HORRID FACE.

There was a little girl,
Who had a little curl,
Right in the middle of her forehead.
When she was good, she was very, very good,
But when she was bad, she was horrid.

RECITE A LINE WITH EACH SWEEP OF THE BRUSH.

One for a tangle,
One for a curl,
One for a boy,
One for a girl,
One to make a parting,
One to tie a bow,
One to brush the cobwebs out
And one to make it grow.

GETTING DRESSED IS FUN
WITH A RHYME TO HELP YOU.

Socks and shoes,
Socks and shoes,
Stripes and spots,
Reds and blues,
Boots for rain,
Boots for snow,
Slip them on
And off we go!

A GOOD RHYME FOR BEDTIME.

A lick of soap for fingers,
A spot of soap for toes,
A little wipe for neck and ears,
And cheeks and chin and nose.
Cuddle in the towel,
Little sleepyhead,
Just brush your teeth
And comb your hair
And snuggle into bed.

USE YOUR HANDS AS BIRDS AND YOUR SHOULDERS AS THE WALL.
THE BIRDS FLY AWAY BEHIND YOUR BACK.

Two little dickeybirds
Sitting on a wall,
One named Peter,
One named Paul.
Fly away, Peter,
Fly away, Paul,
Come back, Peter,
Come back, Paul.

Piggy on the railway,
Picking up the stones.
Along came an engine
And broke poor Piggy's bones.
"Oh!" said Piggy.
"That's not fair."
"Oh!" said the engine driver.
"I don't care."

THIS RHYME IS GOOD FOR DEFUSING TANTRUMS.

ONE HAND ON HIP FOR THE HANDLE, THE OTHER HAND IS THE SPOUT. BEND UP AND DOWN FROM THE WAIST FOR POURING OUT.

I'm a little teapot
Short and stout,
Here's my handle
Here's my spout.
When the water boils
Hear me shout,
Tip me over and pour me out!

A SNACKTIME RHYME.

Jam for dinner,
Honey for tea,
Lots for you and
Lots for me.
Raspberry, strawberry,
Cherry and plum,
With bread and butter,
Yum! Yum! Yum!

RHYMES ARE FUN ON WET DAYS.

It's raining, it's pouring,
the old man is snoring,
He fell out of bed
And bumped his head
And couldn't get up in the morning.

Rain, rain, go away,
Come again another day.

SHAVING IS LIKE A GAME TO A YOUNG CHILD.

There was an old man called Michael Finnigan,
He grew whiskers on his chinnigan,
The wind came out and blew them in again,
Poor old Michael Finnigan,
Begin again.

MAKE EXAGGERATED WOBBLING MOVEMENTS AND LOUD SIZZLING NOISES.

Jell-O on the plate,
Jell-O on the plate,
Wibble, wobble, wibble, wobble,
Jell-O on the plate.

Sausage in the pan,
Sausage in the pan,
Sizzle, sizzle, sizzle, sizzle,
Sausage in the pan.

Monday, washday,
Tuesday, dry day,
Playtime, Wednesday, Thursday, Friday,
Grubby on Saturday,
Rest on Sunday,
Wash, wash, wash, wash,
All day Monday.

SAYING A RHYME WHILE BATHING HELPS TO GET YOU REALLY CLEAN.

HOLD YOUR PALMS UPWARD TO BE SLAPPED
WHEN THE WEASEL POPS!

Half a pound of twopenny rice,
Half a pound of treacle,
That's the way the money goes,
Pop! goes the weasel.

Five currant buns in a baker's shop,
sweet and round with sugar on top,
Along came a boy with a penny one day,
Bought a currant bun and took it right away.

START WITH FIVE FINGERS AND PUT ONE DOWN
EACH TIME A BUN IS TAKEN AWAY UNTIL NONE
ARE LEFT. RECITE A VERSE FOR EACH NUMBER,
FROM FIVE DOWN TO ONE.

One currant bun in a baker's shop,
Sweet and round with sugar on top,
Along came a boy with a penny one day,
Bought that currant bun and took it right away.

How many beans make five?
One bean, two beans,
A bean and a half
And half a bean.

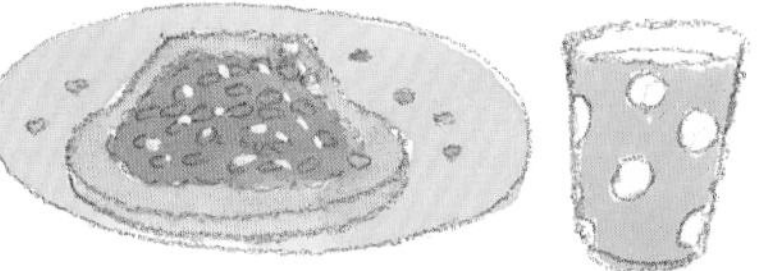

TRADITIONALLY RECITED TO COUNT FRUIT PITS. VERY YOUNG CHILDREN COULD COUNT MOUTHFULS . . . OR CRACKERS OR COOKIES.

Tinker
Tailor
Soldier
Sailor
Rich man
Poor man
Beggar man
Thief.

Curly locks! Curly locks!
Will you be mine?
You shall not wash dishes
Nor yet feed the swine,
But sit on a cushion
And sew a fine seam,
And feed upon strawberries,
Sugar, and cream.

PRETEND YOU ARE RIDING A PONY.

Yankee Doodle went to town,
A-riding on a pony,
Stuck a feather in his hat
And called it macaroni.

BUMP ALONG THE GROUND ON YOUR BOTTOM
AT EACH CHORUS—*BUMPETY, LUMPETY,* IT'S GREAT FUN!

A farmer went trotting upon his gray mare,
BUMPETY, BUMPETY, BUMP!
With his daughter behind him
So rosy and fair,
LUMPETY, LUMPETY, LUMP!
A raven cried, "CROAK!"
And they all tumbled down,
BUMPETY, BUMPETY, BUMP!

The mare banged her knees
And the farmer his crown,
LUMPETY, LUMPETY, LUMP!
The mischievous raven flew laughing away,
BUMPETY, BUMPETY, BUMP!
And vowed he would serve them the same the next day,
LUMPETY, LUMPETY, LUMP!

RING-AROUND-A-ROSY CAN BE ENJOYED BY AS FEW
OR AS MANY AS YOU LIKE.
USE TOYS AS EXTRAS!

Ring-around-a-rosy,
A pocketful of posies,
Ashes! Ashes!
We all fall down.

A cough, a sneeze,
A tissue, please!

A MARCHING RHYME WILL ENCOURAGE YOUR CHILD
UP THE STAIRS TO BED.

Oh, the grand old Duke of York,
He had ten thousand men,
He marched them up to the top of the hill,
And he marched them down again.

And when they were up they were up,
And when they were down they were down,
And when they were only halfway up,
They were neither up nor down.